J   636.9323 R
Rayner, Matthew.
Guinea pig /
32050005896060

WITHDRAWN

D1214171

Guinea Pig

Written by
Matthew Rayner BVetMed MRCVS

Photographed by
Darren Sawyer

Gareth Stevens
Publishing

East Central Regional Library
244 South Birch
Cambridge, Minnesota 55008

Please visit our web site at: www.garethstevens.com
For a free color catalog describing Gareth Stevens
Publishing's list of high-quality books and multi-
media programs, call 1-800-542-2595 (USA) or
1-800-387-3178 (Canada).

Library of Congress Cataloging-in-Publication Data

Rayner, Matthew.
    Guinea Pig / written by Matthew Rayner;
photographed by Darren Sawyer. — North
American ed.
        p. cm. — (I am your pet)
    Includes bibliographical references and index.
    Summary: Presents simple information about
guinea pigs and choosing one as a pet.
    ISBN 978-0-8368-8385-5 (lib. bdg.)
    1. Guinea pigs as pets—Juvenile literature.
I. Sawyer, Darren, ill. II. Title.
SF459.G9R39   2008
636.935'92—dc22   2007010911

This North American edition first published in 2008 by
Gareth Stevens Publishing
A Weekly Reader Company
1 Reader's Digest Road
Pleasantville, NY 10570–7000 USA

Original edition copyright © 2006 by Bookwork Ltd.,
Unit 17, Piccadilly Mill, Lower Street, Stroud,
Gloucestershire, GL5 2HT, United Kingdom.

This edition copyright © 2008 by Gareth Stevens, Inc.

Editorial Director: Louise Pritchard
Senior Editor: Annabel Blackledge
Design Director: Jill Plank
Senior Art Editor: Kate Adams
Consultant: Caroline Reay BVSc Cert VR MRCVS,
    chief veterinary surgeon at The Blue Cross animal
    hospital, Merton, UK

Gareth Stevens Editor: Alan Wachtel
Gareth Stevens Designers: Kami Strunsee and
    Scott M. Krall

All photographs by Darren Sawyer
(www.sawyersphoto.com)

The publishers thank Nikki and Rex Matthews for
supplying guinea pig models for this book.

All rights reserved. No part of this publication may be
reproduced, stored in a retrieval system, or transmitted
in any form or by any means, electronic, mechanical,
photocopying, recording, or otherwise, without the prior
written permission of the copyright holder.

Printed in the United States of America

1 2 3 4 5 6 7 8 9 11 10 09 08 07

It's time
we learned how
to read!

Contents

Words that appear in the glossary are printed in **boldface** type the first time they are used in the text.

Family ties

I am one of the many types of guinea pigs people keep as pets. Some people call me a guinea pig, and others call me a cavy. I come from a large family of animals called **rodents**. I am related to mice, hamsters, and rats.

Surprising speed

I may not look like I can move fast, but I can run very quickly if I want to. I can also stand up and scamper around with surprising speed.

All about me

Shy but sweet

I am often nervous, and I get a little scared in open spaces. If you are calm and gentle with me and let me get used to you slowly, I will quickly become braver.

Tough teeth

Like other rodents, I have teeth that never stop growing. I chew and gnaw a lot to keep them from getting too long. If my teeth are too long, I cannot eat properly, and I might get sick.

Tail talk

Unlike most other animals, I do not have a tail. I don't climb as much as other rodents so I do not need a tail for balance.

Hair not fur
My **coat** is rough, so it is called hair, not fur.

I am a small pet. Handle me gently.

Super senses
I can smell and hear much better than you can. My eyesight is very good, too. I notice any quick movements around me — even above my head!

A little help
You will need some help from an adult to take care of me. An adult will make sure we do not hurt each other by mistake.

Coats and colors

Tricolor
The coat of a tricolor guinea pig has three different colors. One of the colors is always white.

American Crested
This kind of guinea pig has a short coat with a swirl of hair at the top of its head.

It takes all kinds

All guinea pigs are about the same shape and size, but our coats come in many patterns, colors, lengths, and styles. There are about twenty-five kinds, or breeds, of guinea pigs that people keep as pets.

Where's the hair?
Hairless and Baldwin guinea pigs have almost no hair. Skinny guinea pigs have hair only on their faces and paws. Guinea pigs without much hair need special care in the cold.

Hair care

Guinea pigs can have short, long, or curly hair. Because short-haired guinea pigs need less **grooming**, they are the easiest to care for.

Rex
These guinea pigs have short, curly coats and curly whiskers.

Coronet
The Coronet guinea pig has very long hair all over its body.

Mixed-breeds
Not every guinea pig is only one breed. Many of us are mixtures of breeds. We are known as mixed-breeds, and we make beautiful pets.

I think I would like a new hairstyle.

Is it safe? I'm coming out to play!

My wild cousins

Wild guinea pigs live in Peru and Bolivia, which are countries in South America. They live in groups and eat grass and other plants. Wild guinea pigs nest between rocks or in **burrows** left behind by other animals.

Nature's way

Part of the gang
My wild cousins depend on each other for warmth, company, and safety. They also warn each other when they sense danger.

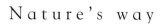

Safe hole
Wild guinea pigs are hunted by other animals and need safe hiding places. I need a place to hide in, too. A **nesting box** or a pile of soft **hay** is a good place.

LOOK OUT!
- **Never chase me.** I might get confused and think you are hunting me. I will be scared and will try to run for cover. I could hurt myself or get very upset or sick.

Wild instincts
I am the same as a wild guinea pig in many ways. I like to spend lots of time nibbling plants and nesting, and I need the company of other guinea pigs. Also like my wild cousins, I am most active early in the morning and just before dark.

Happy in hay
Like my wild relatives, I love to hide in long grass and hay. It makes me feel safe.

All I need

Just the basics
Before you bring me home, you need to get me a hutch, a nesting box, and a **run** to play in. I will also need a litter box and litter, a food bowl and food, a water bottle, **bedding**, and a friend to keep me company.

Bottle and bowl
I need a large drip-feed water bottle. If you put my water in a bowl, I will make a big mess. I also need a food bowl that I cannot tip over or chew up.

It is time for a nap, I think.

Best nest
My nesting box should be cozy but not too small. Make sure the opening is wide enough for me.

Outdoors or indoors?

If I live outdoors, my hutch needs to be strong enough to keep me safe from other animals and bad weather. Place my hutch in a shady, sheltered spot. If I live indoors, keep my hutch away from sunlight and radiators.

Hot and cold
Whether I live indoors or outdoors, I do not want to get too hot, too cold, or damp. I need dry bedding in winter and lots of shade in summer.

Home, sweet home
Get the largest hutch you have space for. One with large doors or a removable roof is the handiest. A hutch with different places to explore will keep me busy.

Bedding down
Line the floor of my hutch with wood shavings and line my litter box with paper- or wood-based litter. Hay is the best nesting material, because I can eat it.

Wood shavings

Wood-based litter

Hay

Pick a piggy

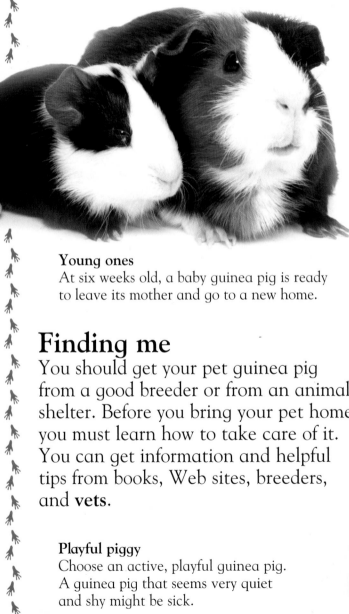

Pick a pair
I will be happiest if I live with another guinea pig. If I am lonely, I might get sick. Just make sure we are either both boys or both girls.

Signs of good health
Be sure you pick a healthy guinea pig. My coat, eyes, ears, nose, and mouth should all be clean.

Young ones
At six weeks old, a baby guinea pig is ready to leave its mother and go to a new home.

Finding me
You should get your pet guinea pig from a good breeder or from an animal shelter. Before you bring your pet home, you must learn how to take care of it. You can get information and helpful tips from books, Web sites, breeders, and **vets**.

Playful piggy
Choose an active, playful guinea pig. A guinea pig that seems very quiet and shy might be sick.

Boars and sows

When you are picking a pet guinea pig, ask an adult to help you learn which ones are boys and which ones are girls. Male guinea pigs are called **boars.** Female guinea pigs are called **sows.**

Who's that climbing over my tunnel?

LOOK OUT!

- **Do not choose** a guinea pig that has been living in a damp, dirty, or crowded hutch. The animal might be sick.
- **Never buy** a guinea pig with a runny nose, runny eyes, bald spots, or diarrhea.

Food and drink

Feed me!

I love to eat. It is my favorite way to pass the time! Make sure I always have a good supply of hay to nibble on. Hay keeps my tummy and my teeth healthy. It is the most important part of my diet.

Green, green grass
I need to eat fresh grass every day, if possible. I will happily spend the day munching away in a run on the lawn.

LOOK OUT!
- **Never feed me** grass clippings. They can make my tummy fill up with gas, and I could get sick.
- **Do not give** me rabbit food. It does not contain all the **vitamins** I need, and it can make me sick.

Eating grass and hay makes me thirsty!

Drink up!
I need fresh water at all times. Rinse my water bottle and change the water every day. Also check that the spout on my bottle is not blocked.

Vitamin C
I need lots of vitamin C in my diet. Grass, fruit, and vegetables contain some vitamin C. You can also add vitamin drops to my water.

A balanced diet
Feed me some guinea pig pellets or mix every day. The package will tell you how much to give me. I also need a handful of fresh fruit or vegetables, but do not overfeed me, or I will get fat.

Chow time
Give me pellets or mix every morning and fruit or vegetables every evening. I look forward to mealtimes. I might even squeak when I hear you coming!

Pellets

Cucumber

Lettuce

Broccoli and cauliflower

Guinea pig mix

Clean up

A clean, dry hutch with plenty of fresh bedding will keep me happy and healthy. Damp bedding can make my paws sore. It also makes it hard for me to breathe. Dirty bedding attracts flies and germs that can make me sick.

Squeaky clean

Daily hay
Give me fresh hay every day. I will not eat damp or dirty hay.

LOOK OUT!
• **Do not use** scented wood shavings in my hutch. They could give me breathing problems.
• **Clean my hutch** more often in warm weather to help keep flies away.

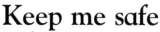

Keep me safe

Make sure you put me in a safe place while you clean my hutch. I will be fine in a pet carrier for a short time, but if the weather is nice, I will be happier outside in my run.

A clean home is a happy home!

Clean often

Remove dirty or wet bedding and any uneaten food from my hutch every day. Give the hutch a full cleaning at least once a week. Clean it even more often if it starts to smell.

Sweep it
Sweep or scoop dirty bedding and food out of my hutch and throw it away.

Empty it
Empty my litter box every time you clean out my hutch. Empty it more often if it gets very dirty.

Wipe it
Wipe my hutch and my litter box with a damp cloth. When they are dry, put in fresh bedding and litter.

Litter training
As long as my hutch is big enough, I will keep my eating, sleeping, and toilet areas separate. If you put a litter box in my hutch, I will quickly get used to using it.

Well groomed

If you see me grooming myself, it means I am feeling relaxed. I also groom my guinea pig friends to show them I like them. If I try to groom you, it means I like you, too!

Tough talk

I usually get along with other guinea pigs, but I might fight if I feel scared or threatened. If you hear me chattering my teeth or hissing, I am about to fight.

What I say

How I "talk"

If you spend enough time with me, you will learn to understand what I am trying to say. Guinea pigs "talk" to others using a mixture of **body language** and sounds.

Leave me alone

If I want to be left alone, I will make a chattering or rumbling noise and try to hide from you. I will push up with my head when you touch me. When I want you to pet me, I will stretch out in front of you and make quiet grunting sounds.

Do I smell food?

Curious creature
When I am curious, I hold my head up high and sniff the air. I might also grunt. When I sense danger, my teeth chatter.

Having fun
When I am happy and having fun, I will run around with my guinea pig friends, and we will touch noses. I might even jump, squeak, and grunt!

LOOK OUT!
- **If I am sitting** with my body all hunched up, and I do not seem to want to play, I might be sick.
- **Listen carefully** to the sounds I make. If I squeak very loudly, I might be in pain.

Scared signs
If I am a little scared, I will try to hide. If I am very scared, I will stay still. I will hold my body very stiff and make loud squeaking noises.

Getting to know you

I can be very shy at first. As I get used to you, I will become more relaxed. Be patient and let me make friends with you slowly. It will be well worth the wait!

Gently does it
Pick me up gently. Slide one hand under my body and hold me steady with the other. Hold me close to your body when you carry me around.

Hold me close

Tempting treats

Giving me treats is a good way to win my trust. Hold the treat out to me with your hand and wait for me to come and get it. Pretty soon, I will come running every time I hear you opening the package!

Gentle nature

I am very gentle, so it is unusual for me to bite or scratch. If I try to bite you when you pick me up or touch me, it probably means I am frightened or in pain.

> I will do anything for a bite of banana!

Dried fruit mix

Guinea pig treats

Healthy nibbles

Give me only small amounts of healthy treats, or I will get too fat.

LOOK OUT!
- **Always hold** me carefully, using both hands. If I struggle or fall, I might hurt myself.
- **Never squeeze** me around my tummy. If you do, you could seriously hurt me.

Keep me busy

As long as I live in a large hutch with at least one other guinea pig, I will not get bored. Give me lots of attention and interesting things to nibble on. If you let me out often to play, I will be a very happy guinea pig!

Lots to do

Pet-store toys
I love toys I can chew on and toys you can stuff with grass or hay. They keep me busy, and they are good for my teeth.

Homemade toys
I do not need expensive toys. An empty toilet-paper roll stuffed with hay will keep me happy for hours!

Talk to me
I am very friendly, and I like to talk. Stop and say hello when you pass my hutch. I will be happy to see you. I might even squeak "hello" back to you!

Room to roam

I enjoy getting exercise and fresh air in a safe run out in the yard or exploring a safe area in your house, but, wherever I am, I need a shelter to hide in.

LOOK OUT!

- **Make sure** that my run is safe from cats and dogs.
- **If you let me** run free in the house, keep electric wires and poisonous plants out of my reach so I do not chew them.

Health check

Paw check
Check my paws to make sure my claws are not too long, and the pads of my feet are not sore.

Getting to know me
If you spend lots of time with me, you will be able to tell when I am not feeling well. If my behavior changes and you are worried about me, talk to the vet.

Coat check
Groom me every day and check my coat and my skin for sores and bald spots.

Daily care
The best way to keep me healthy is to watch me very carefully. Check me over every day when you pick me up. If you notice anything unusual or are worried about me for any reason, take me to the vet.

Bottom check
My bottom should be clean and dry. If it looks dirty or sore, have the vet check it.

Clear ears
My ears should be nice and clean. If you see me scratching them a lot, I might have **mites**. Do not put anything in my ears unless the vet tells you to.

Eyes and nose
Check that my eyes are not runny, cloudy, or closed. My nose should not be runny, either. If you see me sneezing a lot, take me to the vet.

Twigs are really tasty!

Chew check
My teeth never stop growing so I need to chew things to keep them from getting too long. Check inside my mouth to make sure my gums are not sore and my teeth are not too long.

LOOK OUT!
- **If I stop** eating or start drooling, it might be because my teeth are too long.
- **Take me** to the vet as soon as you can if I am unusually quiet or stop eating or drinking. I might have an upset tummy.

Other pets

I am a friendly animal, and I will get along with most other pets. They may not get along with me at first, so introduce us carefully. Never trust a cat or a dog around me. It might think I look like dinner!

Bunny buddy

I like rabbits, but it is not a good idea to leave us alone together. Rabbits like to play rough and can kick hard.

Two's company

LOOK OUT!

• **Guinea pigs** sometimes bully each other. If you see my hutch mates pulling out my hair or fighting with me, ask the vet for some advice. I might become unhappy or sick if I am being bullied.

You and me

If you take good care of me and treat me gently, we will become very good friends.

I don't like to be alone

Like my wild cousins, I need lots of company. I feel lonely and unhappy when I have to spend too much time by myself. When I am unhappy, I am more likely to get sick.

Best friends

Other guinea pigs make the best friends for me. We can live together and be company for each other when you are not around. Just remember that if you keep boars and sows together, you will end up with lots of baby guinea pigs!

Peaceful meeting
The best way to introduce me to other guinea pigs is just to put us in a hutch together. Make sure we each have a place to hide if we need it.

Are you sure there's room in here for two?

Yes, just breathe in and snuggle up!

Babies on board
When a female guinea pig is close to giving birth, she is very big and has trouble moving around. She will need extra food and must be handled with care.

Little piggies

Having babies
Sows can start having babies when they are only three weeks old, and they should always have their first babies before they are eight months old. Guinea pigs usually have three or four babies at a time, but some have only one or as many as eight!

Think carefully
Let your guinea pig have babies only if you can find good homes for all of them. The vet can give your pet an operation to keep it from having babies.

Newborn piggy
A baby guinea pig is born with hair, claws, and teeth. Its eyes are open, and it can move around. Its mother gives it milk and warmth.

Wow! My baby is getting big!

Growing up

Soon after a baby guinea pig is born, it starts to nibble adult food. By the time it is three weeks old, it does not need its mother's milk at all. When guinea pigs are three weeks old, you need to separate the sows from the boars to keep them from having more babies.

Leaving home

Guinea pigs are ready to leave their mothers when they are about six weeks old. Then they can go to new homes!

Glossary

bedding
The soft material used to make a guinea pig's hutch warm and comfortable is called bedding.

boars
Boars are male guinea pigs.

body language
Guinea pigs use body movements to show what they are thinking and feeling. These movements are called body language.

burrows
Some animals make holes or tunnels in the ground to live in and to keep them safe from enemies. The holes or tunnels are often called burrows.

coat
An animal's hair or fur is known as its coat.

grooming
Brushing an animal's coat to keep it clean is called grooming.

hay
Hay is dried grass. It is a healthy food for many animals.

mites
Mites are tiny, insect-like animals that live on other animals and often carry diseases.

nesting box
A small container inside a guinea pig's hutch is filled with bedding to make a warm, cozy nest where pet guinea pigs can sleep or hide.

rodents
Guinea pigs, mice, rats, hamsters, and gerbils all belong to a family of animals called rodents.

run
A run is an enclosed outdoor area where a pet can safely exercise and eat.

sows
Sows are female guinea pigs.

vets
Short for "veterinarians," vets are doctors who take care of animals.

vitamins
Some nutrients, or substances in food that keep animals healthy, are called vitamins.

Find out more . . .

Web Sites

guineapigfun.com
Games, drawings, songs, videos, photos, and fun are only a few of the features on this cavy-crazy Web site.

jackiesguineapiggies.com/ guineapigsounds.html
If you listen carefully to the recordings on this site, you will hear many of the sounds guinea pigs make. You can also read about what the sounds mean.

www.guineapig cages.com
This site tells you just about everything you need to know about guinea pig cages. It also has lots of information about how to keep guinea pigs happy and healthy.

Books

Guinea Pigs and Other Rodents. Bobbie Kalman (Crabtree)

Little Guinea Pigs. Born to Be Wild (series). Anne Royer (Gareth Stevens)

Pet Guinea Pigs. Pet Pals (series). Julia Barnes (Gareth Stevens)

I know you will want to learn more about me!

Index